We Are Citizens of the World

Dewayne Hotchkins

Rosen REAL READERS

Rosen Classroom™
New York

I

My name is Felicia.

I am a citizen of the United States.

I love to play sports.

My favorite sport to play is soccer.

The World Cup is a
soccer tournament.
Teams from all over the world
play in the World Cup.
I like watching the World Cup.

The American team
is my favorite.
I hope they win the World Cup!

This is my friend Pedro.

Pedro lives in Mexico.

He is a Mexican citizen.

Pedro likes the Mexican team.

Mexico is south
of the United States.
Soccer is very popular in Mexico.
In Mexico, soccer is called *fútbol*.

My teacher Mr. Wei is from China.
Mr. Wei likes the Chinese team.

China is a large country
in eastern Asia.
More people live there
than in any other country.
Many people in China love soccer.

People from all over the world watch the World Cup. People like to wear the colors of their favorite team.

We all come from different places.
We like different things, too.
Even though we are not the same,
we are all citizens of the world.

Words to Know

China

Mexico

soccer

teacher

world

World Cup